I Broke My Arm

by Lisa M. Herrington

Content Consultant

Catherine A. Dennis, N.P.

Reading Consultant

Jeanne M. Clidas, Ph.D.
Reading Specialist

Children's Press®
An Imprint of Scholastic Inc.
New York Toronto London Auckland Sydney
Mexico City New Delhi Hong Kong
Danbury, Connecticut

Library of Congress Cataloging-in-Publication Data
Herrington, Lisa M.
 I broke my arm/by Lisa M. Herrington.
    pages cm. — (Rookie read-about health)
Summary: "Introduces the reader to what happens when someone breaks a bone
and how it is treated and cared for"— Provided by publisher.
Audience: Ages 3-6
Includes bibliographical references and index.
  ISBN 978-0-531-21037-6 (library binding: alk. paper) — ISBN 978-0-531-21110-6
(pbk.: alk. paper)
1. Arm—Fractures—Juvenile literature. 2. Bones—Juvenile literature. I. Title. II. Series:
Rookie read-about health

 RD557.H47 2015
 617.1'5—dc23   2014035903

Produced by Spooky Cheetah Press
Design by Keith Plechaty

© 2015 by Scholastic Inc.

All rights reserved. Published in 2015 by Children's Press, an imprint of Scholastic Inc.

Printed in China 62

SCHOLASTIC, CHILDREN'S PRESS, ROOKIE READ-ABOUT®, and associated logos
are trademarks and/or registered trademarks of Scholastic Inc.

1 2 3 4 5 6 7 8 9 10 R 24 23 22 21 20 19 18 17 16 15

Photographs: Alamy Images: 30 (Asia Images Group Pte Ltd), 8 (Jose Oto/
BSIP); Dreamstime/Lucidwaters: 20 inset, 31 center bottom; Getty Images: 16
(Blend Images/ERproductions Ltd), 29 center right (Klaus Vedfelt), cover (Stephen
Simpson); Media Bakery: 27 (Driendl Group), 23 (Jasper Cole), 20 main (JGI), 19,
31 bottom (Science Photo Library), 29 bottom right (Sean Justice); Shutterstock,
Inc./alonggorn: 3 top left, 31 top; Thinkstock: 7 (anatols), 12 (Fuse), 29 center left
(Goodshoot), 11 (itsmejust), 29 top right (Jupiterimages), 3 top right (Liquidlibrary), 3
bottom, 31 center top (Mark Kostich), 29 bottom left (monkeybusinessimages), 4, 24,
29 top left (Purestock).

Illustrations by Jeffrey Chandler/Art Gecko Studios!

T____ of Contents

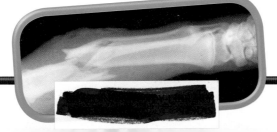

When Your Arm Breaks

Crash! You fall off your bike and hit the ground hard. Your arm hurts so much. You cannot move it. Oh no! You broke your arm.

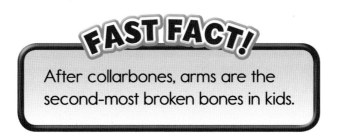

FAST FACT!

After collarbones, arms are the second-most broken bones in kids.

Kids break their arms and wrists a lot. That is because they often put out their hands to stop a fall. Falls and sports injuries are common causes of broken bones.

A bad fall can lead to a broken arm.

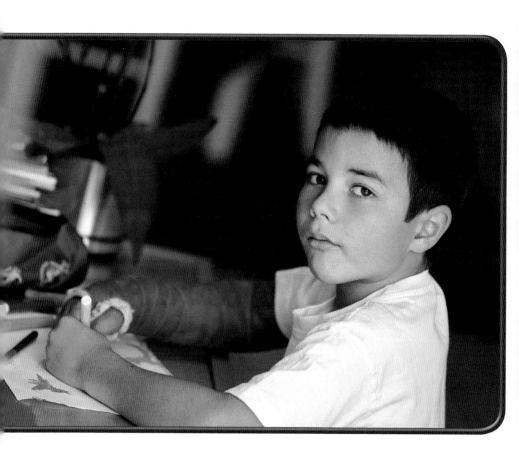

Having a broken arm can be scary. Your bones are amazing, though. Before too long, your arm will heal. It will be strong again.

FAST FACT!

Eating and writing with a broken arm can be hard. You may need to use your other hand until you get better.

How do you know if you broke your arm? Here are some ways you can tell:

- Did you hear a crack or a snap when you hurt yourself?
- Is your arm swollen or bruised?
- Does your arm hurt when you touch it?
- Is it painful to move your arm?

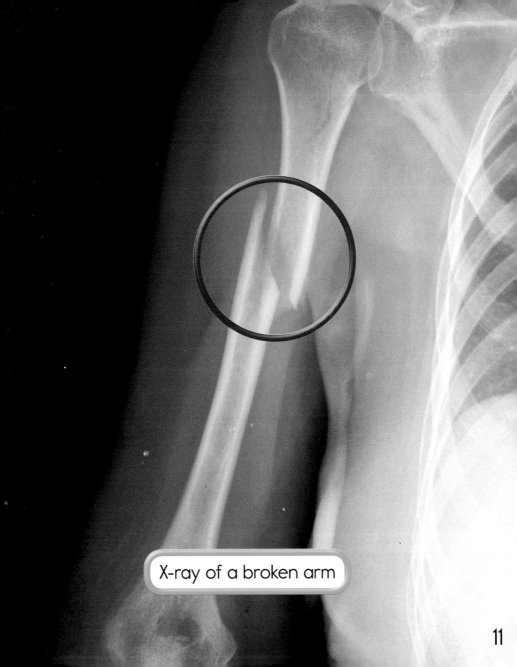

X-ray of a broken arm

What Is a Broken Arm?

Bones support and protect your body. They give your body its shape. Your bones are strong, but they can break. A broken bone is called a **fracture**.

A broken arm can mean a trip to the hospital.

Your arm is made up of three bones. There is one long bone in the upper arm. It is called the humerus (HYOO-mer-us). Two smaller bones are in the lower arm. They are the ulna (UHL-nuh) and radius (RAY-dee-uhs).

Arm bones can break in different ways. For example, a bone can have a crack in it. It can snap in half. It can even shatter into pieces.

Your Arm Bones

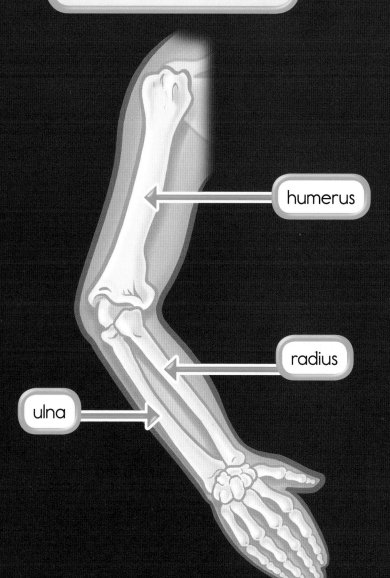

humerus

radius

ulna

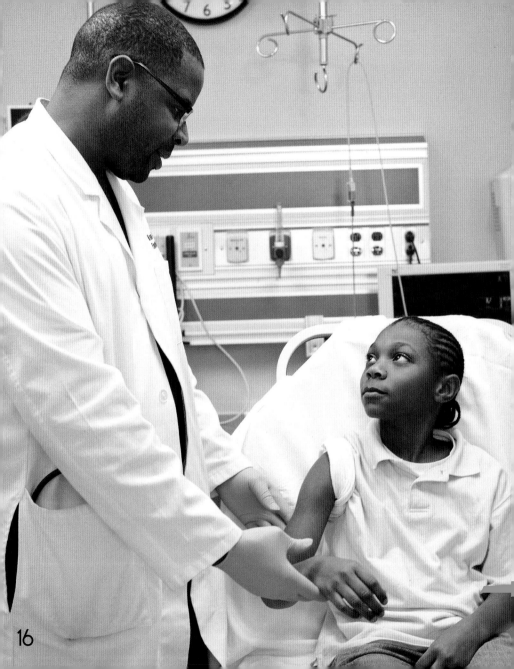

Treating a Broken Arm

If you break your arm, you need to see a doctor. Keep your arm still so the injury does not get worse. Putting an ice pack wrapped in cloth on your arm can help make the swelling go down.

A doctor at the hospital will check your arm. You will get an **X-ray**. This special picture shows how and where your arm is broken. The bone may need to be set. That means the doctor puts the pieces back into place.

An X-ray lets the doctor know how to treat a broken arm.

Most broken arms are put in a **cast**. A cast keeps the bone from moving. Over time, the bone grows back together. You may also get a **sling** to support your arm. More serious breaks may need surgery.

FAST FACT!

Some smaller breaks need only a splint. A splint is like a cast, but it just supports the broken bone on one side.

A broken arm is usually in a cast for about six weeks. Over this time, your arm will get weak. The doctor may tell you to do special exercises after the cast comes off. They will help your arm get its strength back.

FAST FACT!

Kids have softer bones than adults, so their arm bones often do not break completely. The break usually goes through only part of the bone.

Preventing Broken Bones

Eating right makes your bones strong. Strong bones are less likely to break. Your bones need calcium to make them hard. This mineral is found in foods such as milk and cheese.

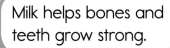

Milk helps bones and teeth grow strong.

Exercise also keeps bones healthy. Kids can break arms playing sports and being active. That is why it is important to wear the right safety gear. Your bones will thank you!

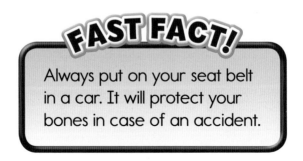

FAST FACT!

Always put on your seat belt in a car. It will protect your bones in case of an accident.

Our bones come in all shapes and sizes. Can you feel the long bone in your arm? What is it called? Find it on the diagram at right. What about the two smaller bones? Do you remember what each is called? Point to them on the diagram.

You have 27 little bones in your hand and wrist. Can you feel them?

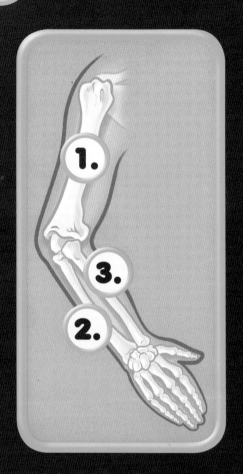

Answers: The long bone in your arm is the humerus. It is number 1 on the diagram. The two smaller bones are the ulna (number 2) and radius (number 3).

Bone Builders

Point to the picture in each pair that shows a good way to keep bones strong and safe.

 1.

 2.

 3.

Answers: 1. Drinking milk helps build strong bones. 2. Wearing a seat belt in the car keeps you safe. 3. Wearing a helmet when riding a scooter helps prevent broken bones.

Strange but True!

Your bones change as you grow. You are born with more than 300 bones. But as you get bigger, some of your bones join together. By the time you are grown, you will have only 206 bones!

Just for Fun

Q: I broke my arm in one place. What should I do?

A: Do not go back to that place again!

Q: How do you make a skeleton laugh?

A: Tickle its funny bone.

Glossary

cast (KAST): hard covering that supports and protects a broken arm

fracture (FRAK-chur): broken or cracked bone

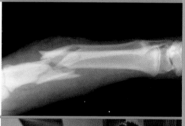

sling (SLING): loop of cloth used to support a broken arm

X-ray (EKS-ray): picture of your bones

Index

Facts for Now

Visit this Scholastic Web site for more information on broken arms:
www.factsfornow.scholastic.com
Enter the keywords **Broken Arm**

About the Author

Lisa M. Herrington is the author of many books and articles for kids. Lisa lives in Trumbull, Connecticut, with her husband, Ryan, and daughter, Caroline. She loves them with every bone in her body!